WHEN CROWS ARE WHITE

WORDS
JERRY PINTO

ART
GARIMA GUPTA

SCHOLASTIC
New York Toronto London Auckland
Sydney New Delhi Hong Kong

IN THE MIDDLE OF THE NIGHT, YOU SOMETIMES WAKE UP BECAUSE THE CROWS SUDDENLY START CAWING LOUDLY, AS IF IN PROTEST.

PERHAPS YOU ASK YOURSELF, 'Why do we have crows?'

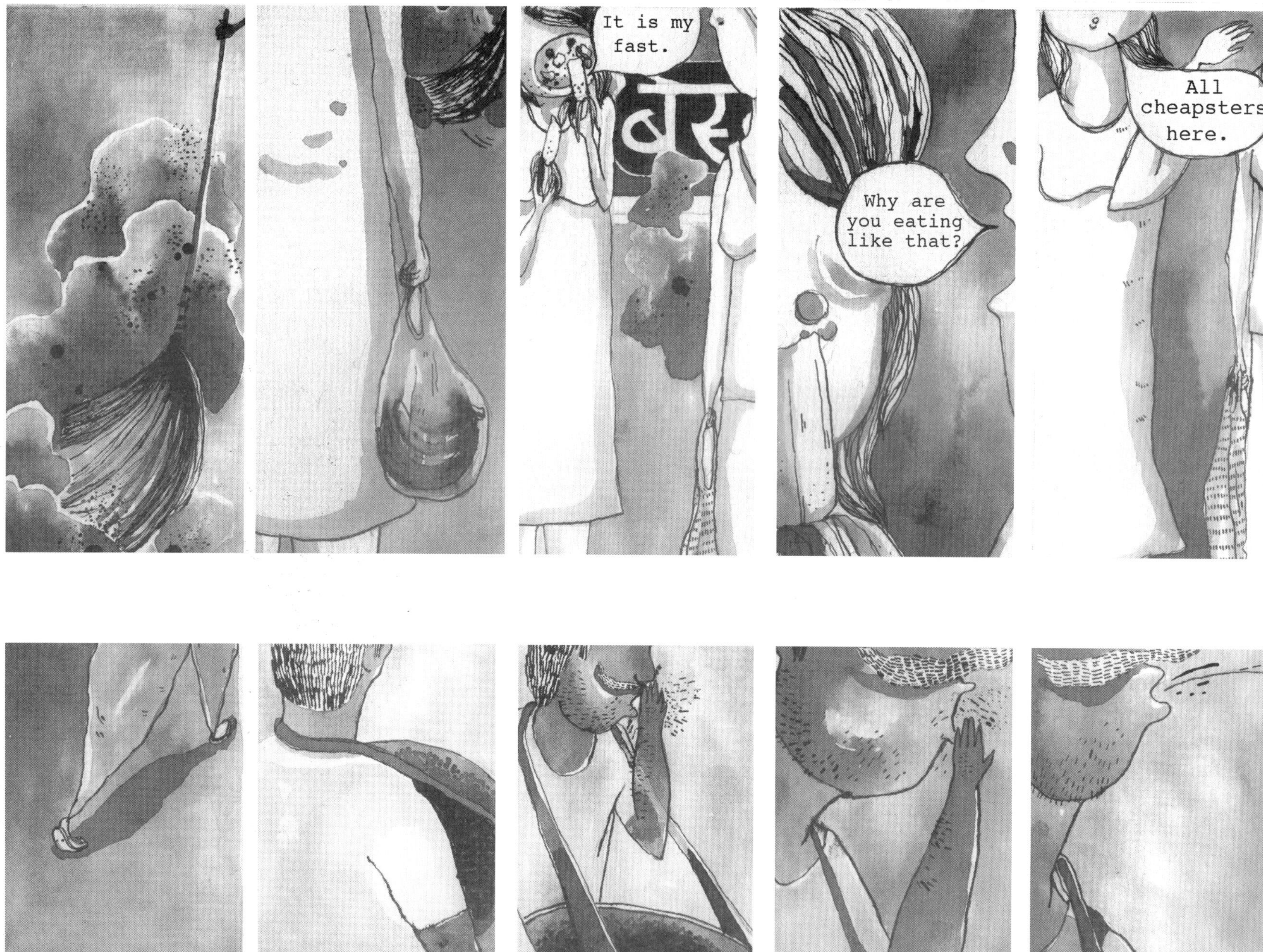
It is my fast.
Why are you eating like that?
All cheapsters here.

SOMETIMES IT'S BETTER NOT TO ASK WHAT A CROW IS EATING.
NOT UNLESS YOU'RE THE POLICE.

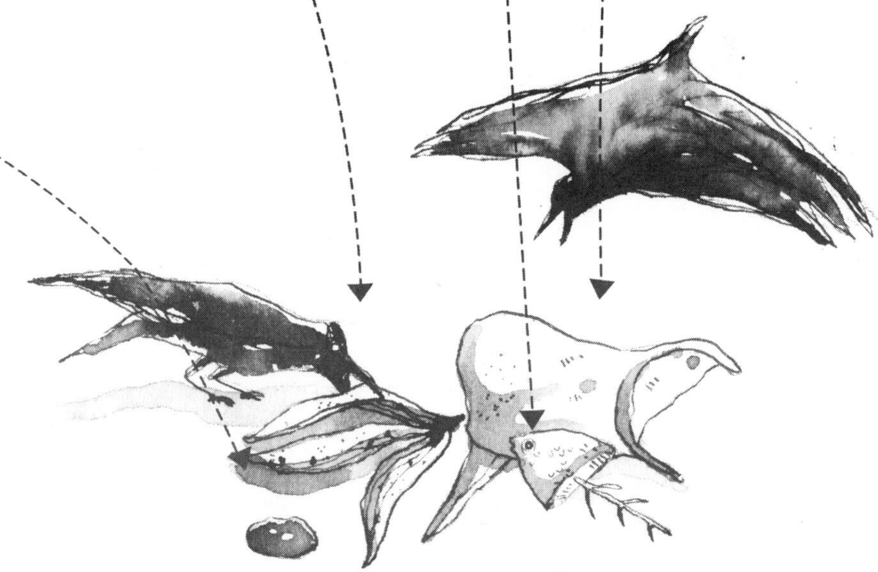

Saawri was asleep and dreaming when the outcry came.

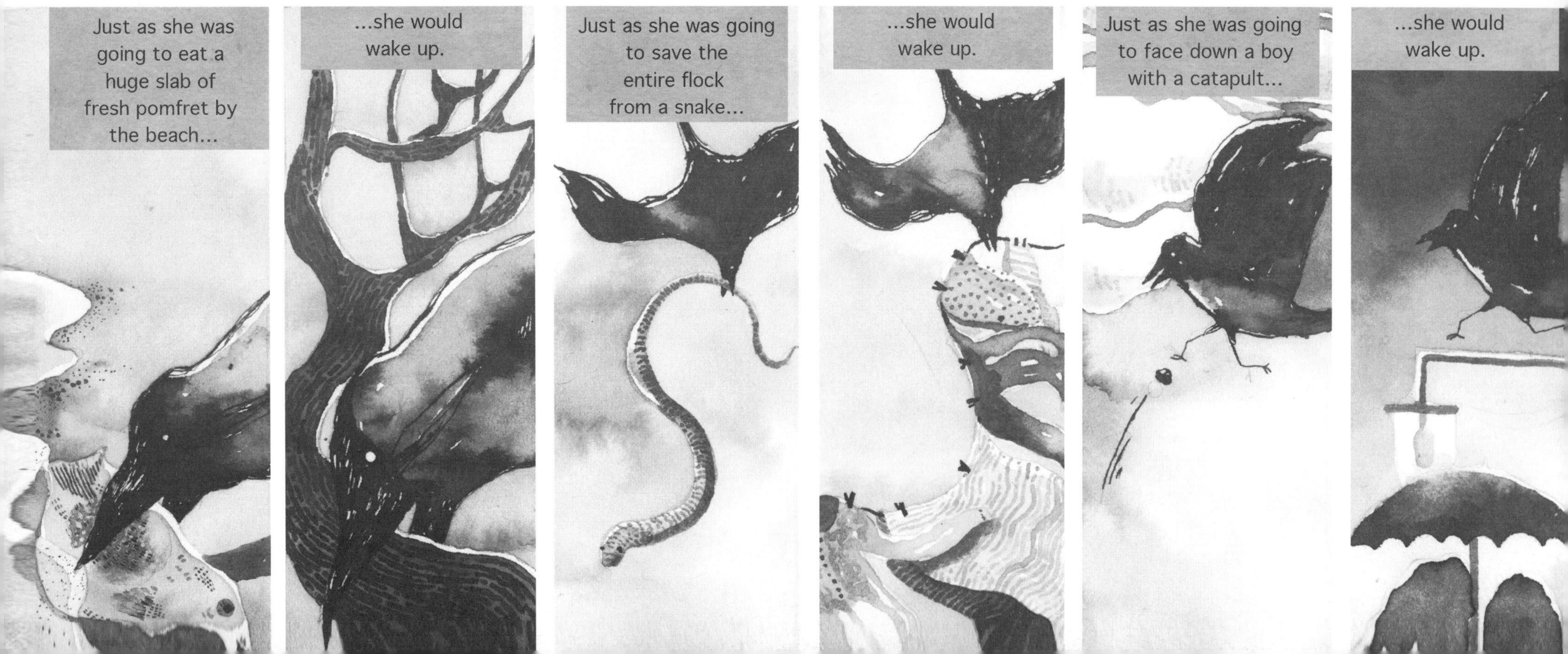

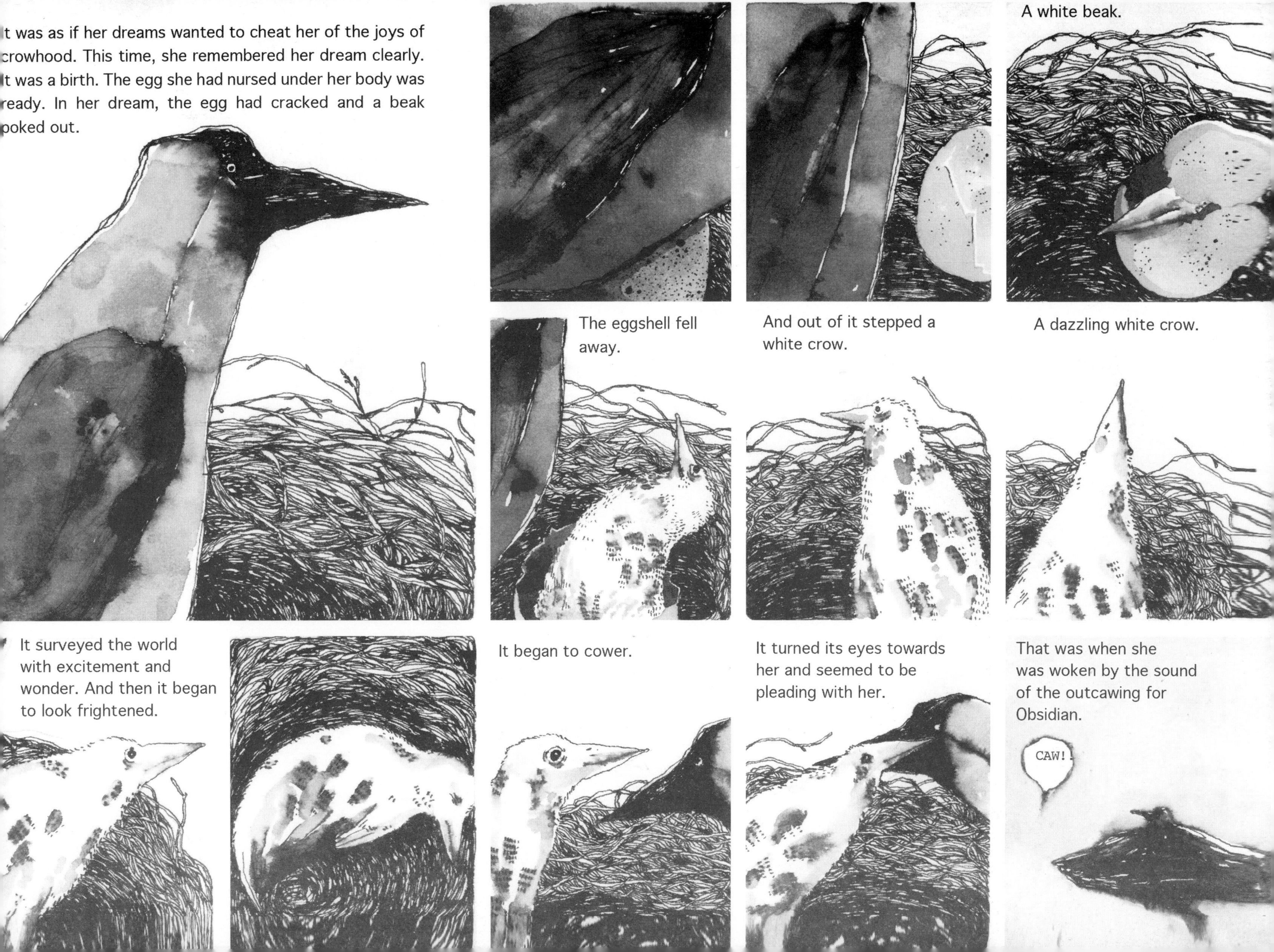
It was as if her dreams wanted to cheat her of the joys of crowhood. This time, she remembered her dream clearly. It was a birth. The egg she had nursed under her body was ready. In her dream, the egg had cracked and a beak poked out.
A white beak.
The eggshell fell away.
And out of it stepped a white crow.
A dazzling white crow.
It surveyed the world with excitement and wonder. And then it began to look frightened.
It began to cower.
It turned its eyes towards her and seemed to be pleading with her.
That was when she was woken by the sound of the outcawing for Obsidian.
CAW!

YOU GO BACK TO SLEEP. YOU SHOULD GET YOUR EIGHT HOURS A NIGHT AND YOU'RE GOING TO BE ALL RIGHT. WELL, ALMOST...

But the crows do not go back to sleep. This is because one of the members of the murder has just died. When a crow dies, all the other crows open their beaks and caw encouragement to the rising spirit crow, its body now perfect, its wings blacker than the black sky. They caw it farewell as its body falls to the ground, to be swept away the next morning and thrown on the garbage dumps where even the dogs ignore it.

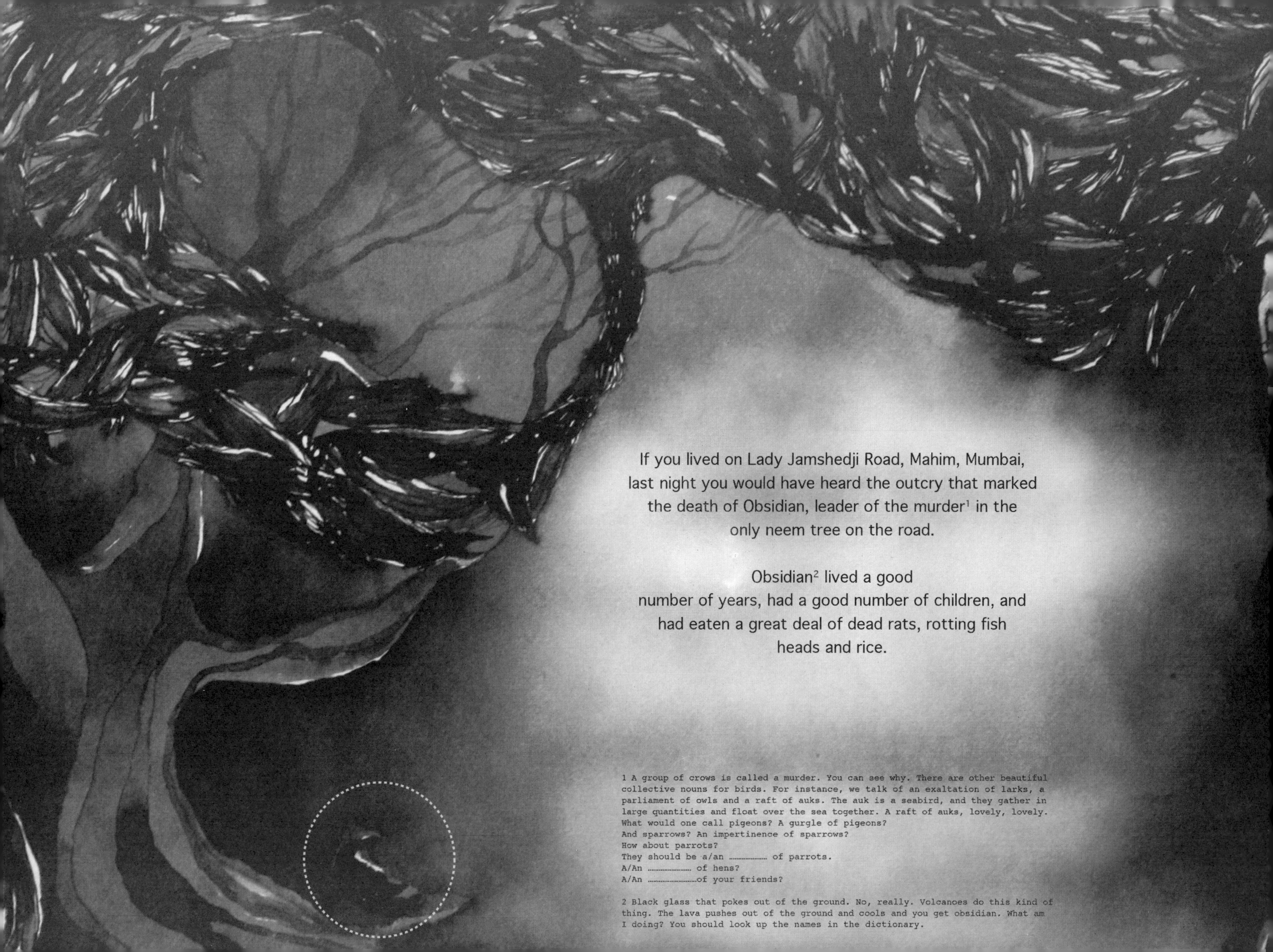

If you lived on Lady Jamshedji Road, Mahim, Mumbai, last night you would have heard the outcry that marked the death of Obsidian, leader of the murder[1] in the only neem tree on the road.

Obsidian[2] lived a good number of years, had a good number of children, and had eaten a great deal of dead rats, rotting fish heads and rice.

1 A group of crows is called a murder. You can see why. There are other beautiful collective nouns for birds. For instance, we talk of an exaltation of larks, a parliament of owls and a raft of auks. The auk is a seabird, and they gather in large quantities and float over the sea together. A raft of auks, lovely, lovely.
What would one call pigeons? A gurgle of pigeons?
And sparrows? An impertinence of sparrows?
How about parrots?
They should be a/an .... of parrots.
A/An .... of hens?
A/An ....of your friends?

2 Black glass that pokes out of the ground. No, really. Volcanoes do this kind of thing. The lava pushes out of the ground and cools and you get obsidian. What am I doing? You should look up the names in the dictionary.

Saawri cawed too, but her heart was not in it. Obsidian had not been a crow chief of any significance at all.

If you asked, 'Why?' Obsidian had a single answer...

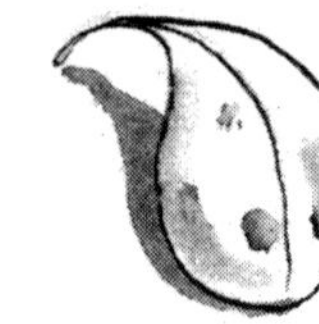

The new chief, she hoped, would be different. Noir[3].

Saawri had hopes for Noir. She had seen him taste broccoli when none of the other crows would touch it.

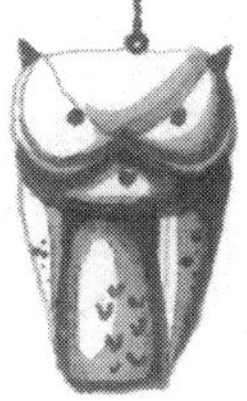

When one of the families in the building across the road had hung out a metal owl to frighten them and stop them from sitting on the clothesline, Noir had flown down and sat on the owl. All the other crows knew the owl was a fake, of course. They could see it was a fake. They could smell it was a fake. But they weren't going to prove it. Noir was the kind who would take a look at a metal owl and decide that everything he knew told him it was a fake. So he would treat it like a fake. He would sit on it to show what he thought of the humans who had put up the owl.

3 Black in French. I put this one in because you might not find it in an English dictionary.

Perhaps Noir would change things.

There was one thing Saawri wanted the crows to change very badly. It was their habit of attacking a wounded crow and killing it. She could not bear it and would fly away from the scene, seeking the shelter of a roof or a clothesline as the murder proceeded. She had once tried singing to herself but discovered that human beings don't like crow song. So now Saawri simply looked the other way.

She knew that was almost as bad as helping kill a wounded crow.

4 Look up the word, you lazy lump. And then look up the word 'euphemism'.

Obsidian laughed and a sparrow
in the next tree almost fainted.

Saawri had heard the story.

WHY CROWS CULL

Once upon a time, in the time when time was so solid things could stand upon it, the shadow of the crow was its soul and its conscience.

The crow enjoyed looking at itself in whatever reflective surface it could find. The crow was vain. Very vain.

The crow's shadow tried
to warn the crow.

But the crow had begun to ignore its shadow.

One day, as the crow was flying to the conference of the birds, it saw a piece of volcanic glass glittering in the distance. Immediately it changed its flight path.

Its shadow shouted...

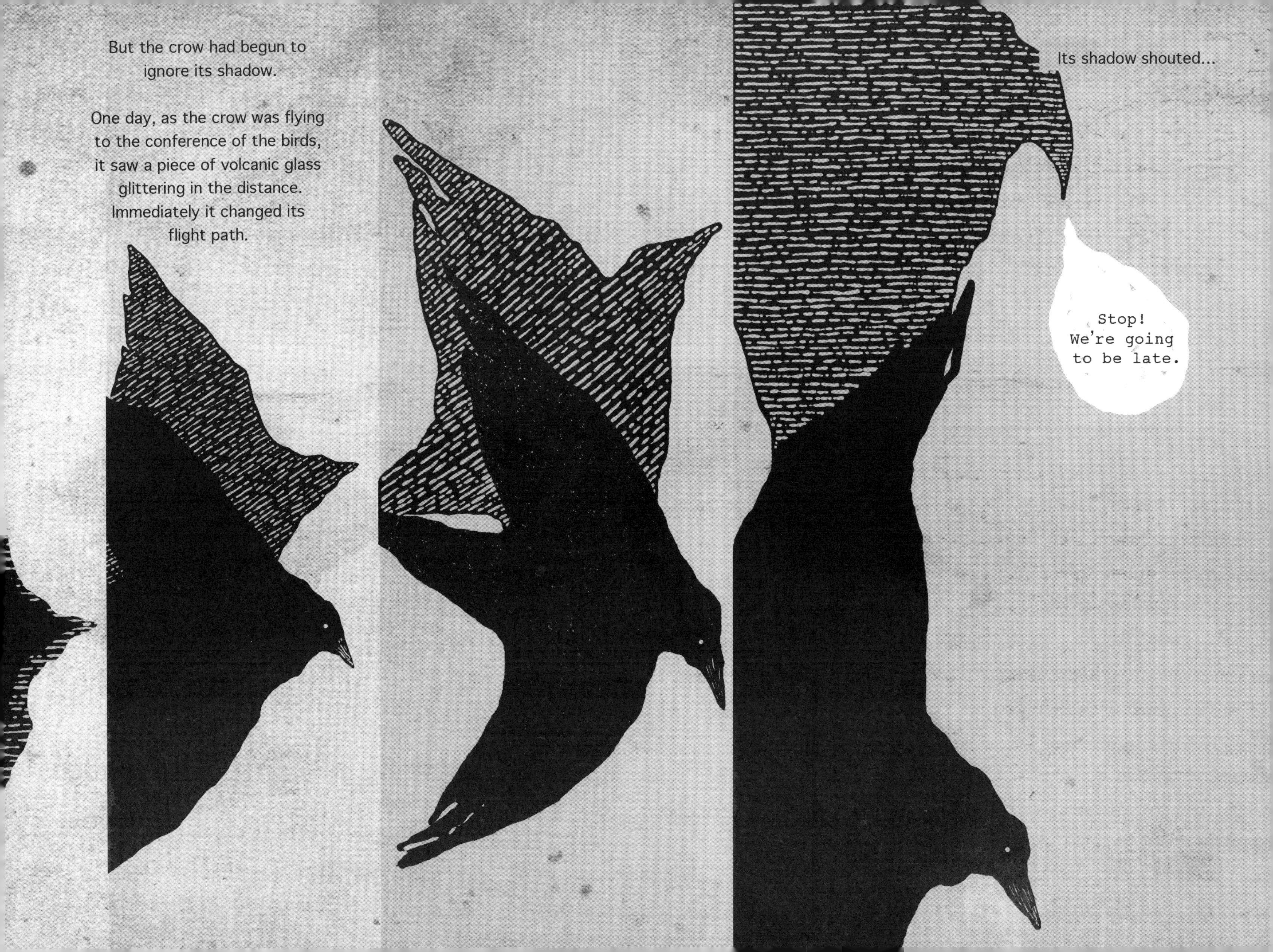

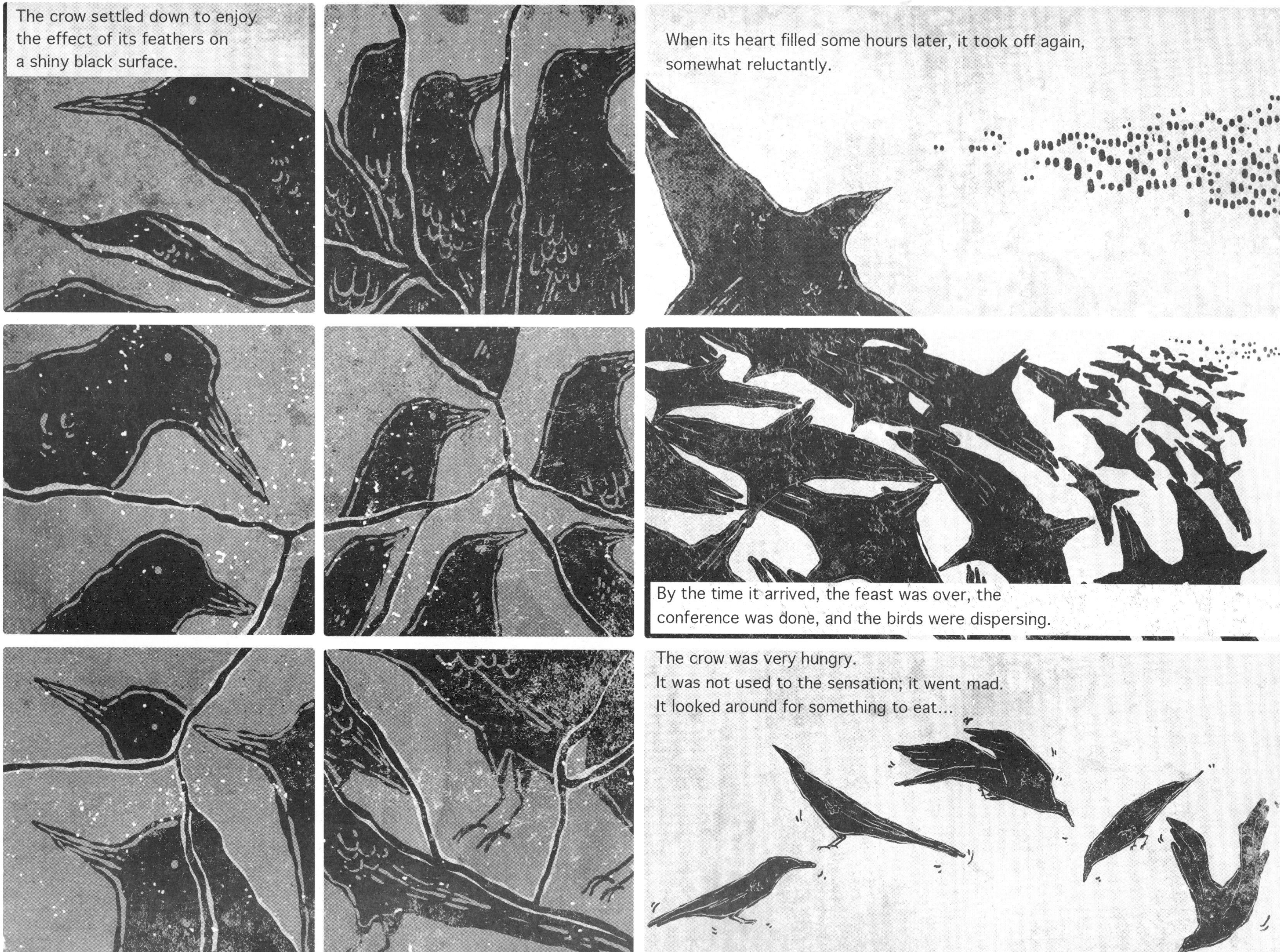
The crow settled down to enjoy the effect of its feathers on a shiny black surface.
When its heart filled some hours later, it took off again, somewhat reluctantly.
By the time it arrived, the feast was over, the conference was done, and the birds were dispersing.
The crow was very hungry.
It was not used to the sensation; it went mad.
It looked around for something to eat...

...and saw an old crow about to die.
What are you doing?
But I'm hungry!
But you cannot feast on the flesh of another of your kind.
Oh can't I?
I am sure there are other things to eat.
You go find them.
Dutifully, the crow's shadow departed to look for food. This was easy because it was night.
And even as it flew away, it heard a terrible sound.
CAW!!!

The young crow had decided to speed things up. It was attacking the old crow. The shadow raced back but it was too late. The crow's beak was wet with blood.
What have you done?

Shut up, shut up or…
Or what?

And Crow set upon Shadow and killed him and ate him up too.

And shadows all over the world lost their substance so that they should not meet the fate that the shadow of the crow met. And since then, crows have attacked each other when they have seen a sign of weakness.

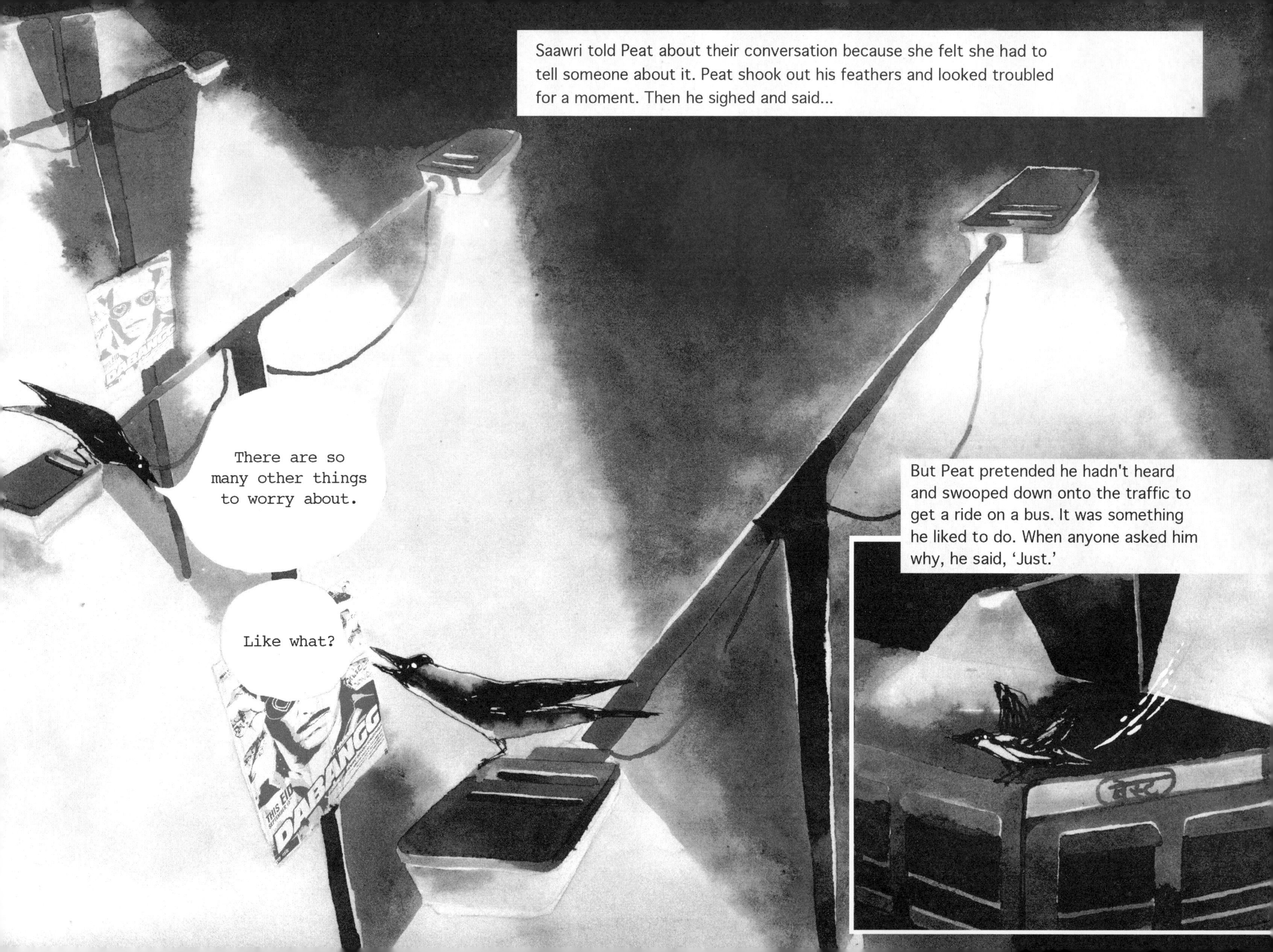
Saawri told Peat about their conversation because she felt she had to tell someone about it. Peat shook out his feathers and looked troubled for a moment. Then he sighed and said...
There are so many other things to worry about.
Like what?
THIS EID
DABANGG
But Peat pretended he hadn't heard and swooped down onto the traffic to get a ride on a bus. It was something he liked to do. When anyone asked him why, he said, 'Just.'

Saawri tried others in the flock and they shrugged her off. There were other more important things to do. Dusqui[5] had to find suitably soft material for her nest and could not stop to discuss it. Liliar[6] laughed and told her to mind her own business and work with her instincts. But Saawri needed more answers.

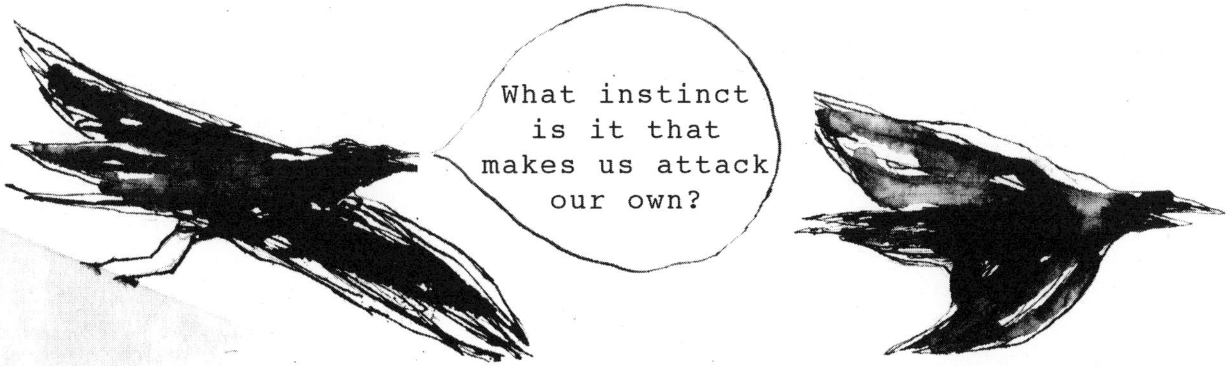

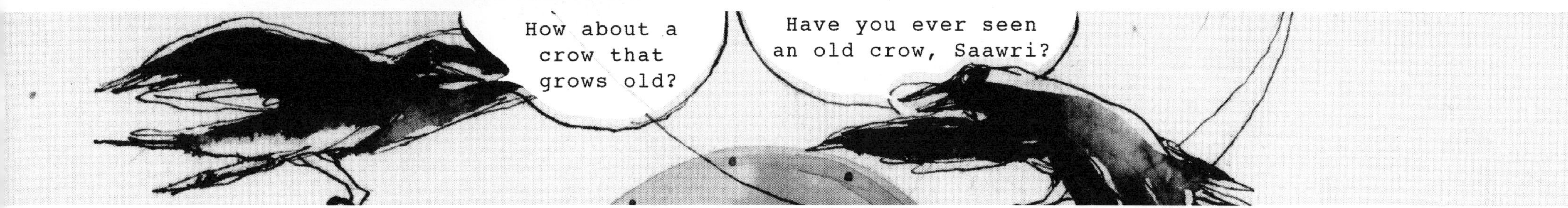

Saawri had no reply to that. Perhaps Noir would be different. Saawri knew she had to act fast because the dream was getting urgent now. The egg would crack and the white crow would step out—extraordinary, alabaster, terrified. Each time, it seemed to be pleading with her, begging her for protection.

But Saawri could think of no way to help. She tried with Grey, one of the elder members of the flock.

5 Okay, her name was actually Dusky, but she likes to spell it this way.

6 Tamil word for a semi-precious stone. What colour is it? What colour do you think it is?

Why is tradition so important to us?
Well, I suspect it's because traditions have survived...
...because there's some reason to them.
I think a society tries several ways and finally figures out one that works.
Then it begins to repeat it and a tradition is formed.
But that means they can be changed?
I should think so, technically, yes, they can, but I think it might be difficult to persuade most crows.

They rather like tradition.
What about a cruel tradition like killing a wounded crow?

But there seemed to be something wrong with this logic.
Saawri also began to realise that she had been hiding her real worries. She tried to think of several ways to broach the subject but none of them worked. How did one mention the unmentionable? How did one say the unsayable? How did one speak of a white crow? Specially when there were stories about why crows are black.

WHY CROWS ARE BLACK

Version 1

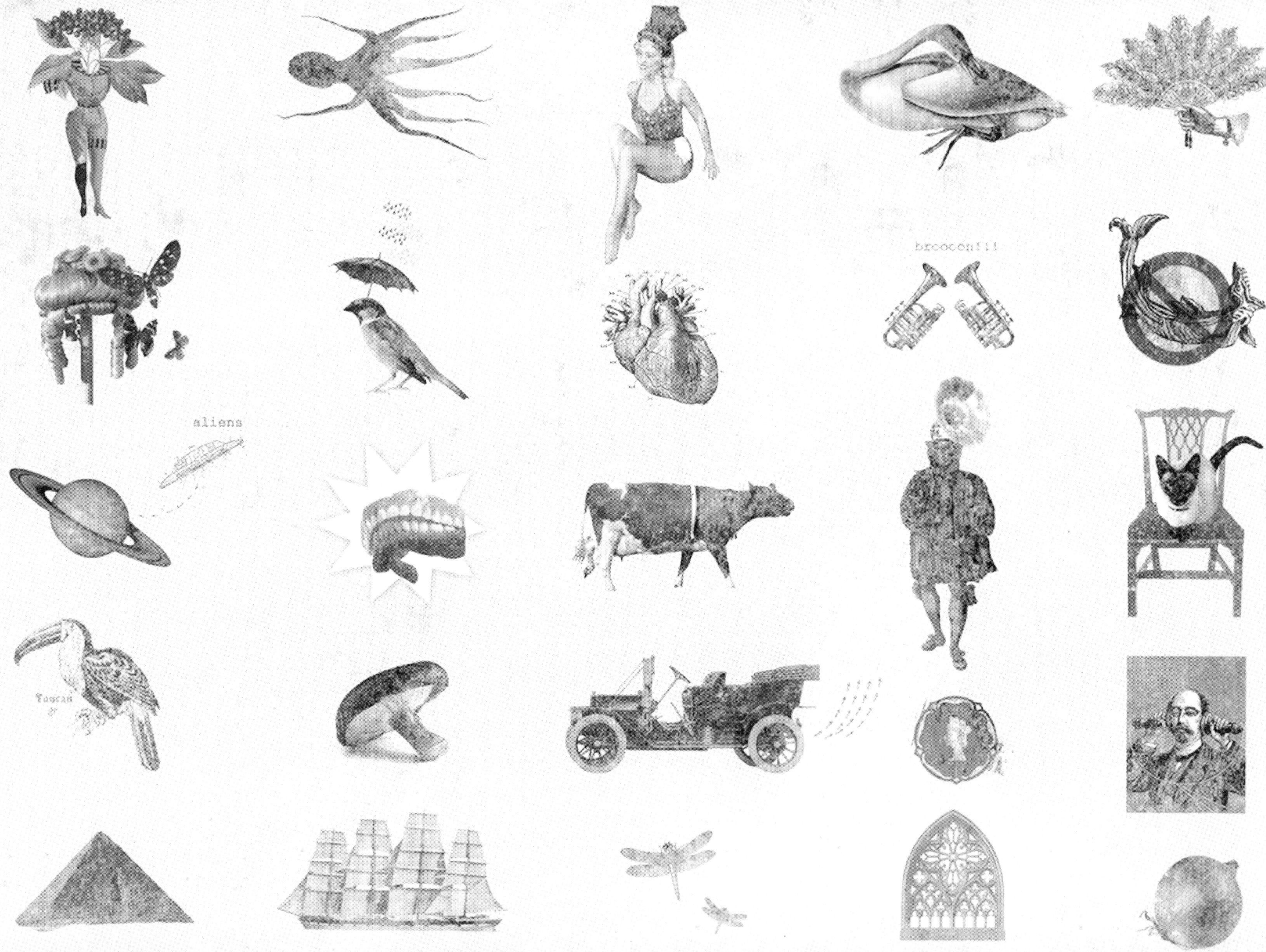
aliens
brooccn!!!
Toucan

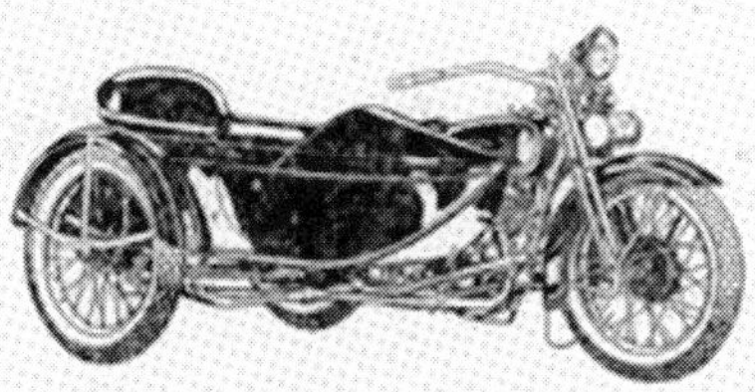

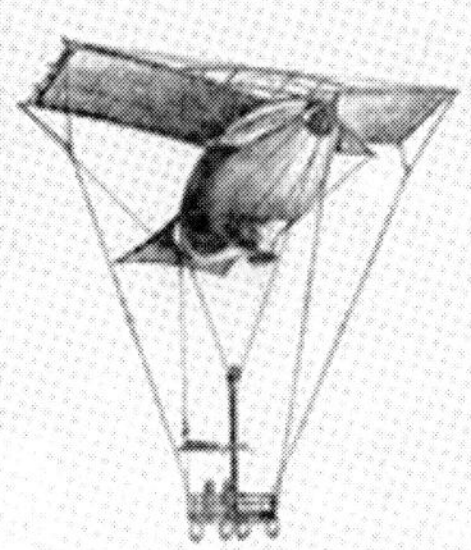

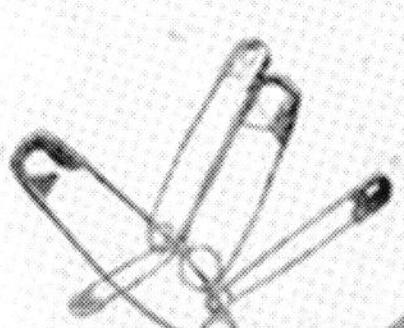

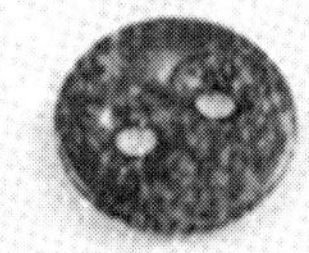

BE

When the world began, it was Kaal who came to the centre of the universe and said, 'Be.'

'Be' was powerful magic.

From it sprang gods and demons, men and cowmen, colour and sound, shape and taste, black mud and great arcs of light, language and music, dogs and blankets, thought and sleep, dreams and facts, coffee and onions, you and me…everything you know and ought to know and will know and would know if you could live long enough.

The great sorting took a cycle of 365 aneya.(Each aneya is as long as 365 earth years.)

And when it was all done, Kaal knew her work was over. She took her sack and began to fold it into a pillow. And inside she felt something small and round and hard.

Already she was beginning to fall asleep when she drew out an egg. Somehow this egg had slipped out of the magic and ended in her sack.

It would miss 2,497,397 aneyas of creation now.

'That's a pity,' she thought.
She tapped it. It opened. And a bird stepped out.

Kaal wanted to invent it properly. But her eyes were already closing and the dark was closing in.

Kaal did not hear her.
The bird hopped closer to the ear of Kaal.

But Kaal was already asleep. Creation was over.
And so it is that crows are black from the sleep
in the eye of time and so it is that their call
is Kaa…

WHY CROWS ARE BLACK

Version 2

Once upon a time, the crow was blue. The prettiest blue. The blue of the sky. With white patches under her wings…
Why? You tell me why. She was, she thought, a good-looking bird because she was blue. But she was unhappy that her eggs were white.

A blue bird should have blue eggs. It stands to reason.

Actually, it didn't. There is no reason for a bird to have eggs of the same colour as her wings. But the crow had become obsessed about the colour of her eggs. One day, she discovered a nest with some blue eggs in it. The eggs were the same colour as the crow's wings.
It was the koel's nest.

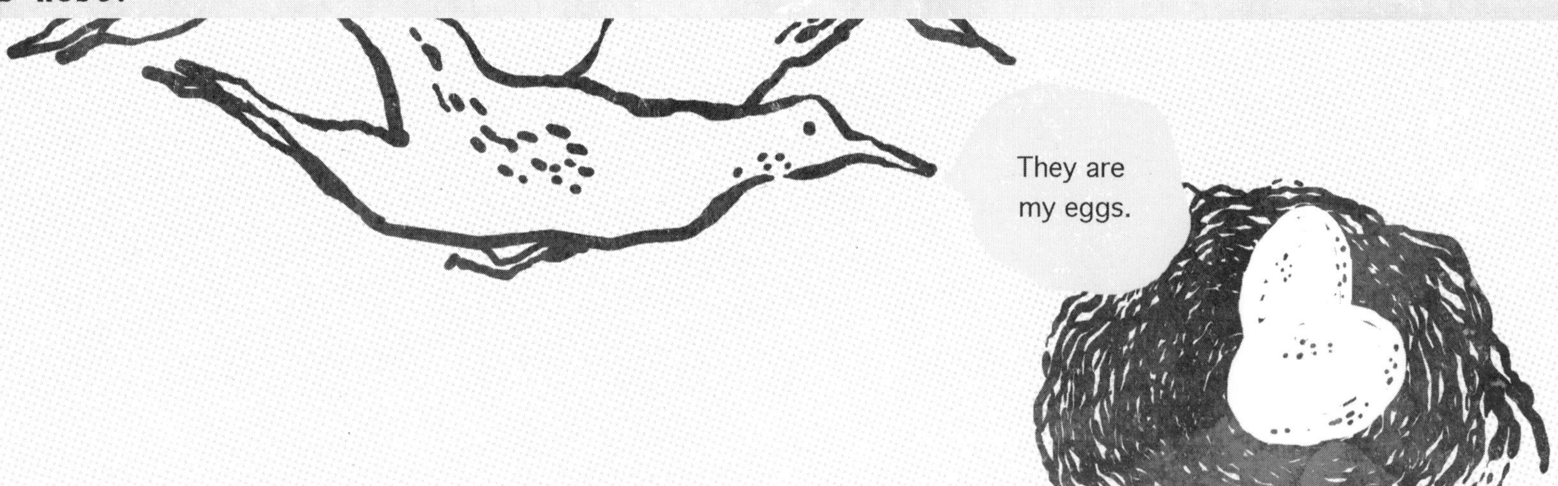

The crow was non-vegetarian, then as now. It had to hunt. Got it? No? You're looking for a quick meal. You spot a nice fat worm. You begin to glide in. Maybe your shadow passes over the worm and the worm turns. He looks up. All it sees is a bit of sky. Get it? That's called camouflage.

And so she hatched a plan. That night she rubbed herself in coal dust until she was black. Then she went to the bottom of the tree where the koel had her nest and she hissed as if she were a snake. The koel took fright and flew into the air. And the crow flew up to the koel's nest. She picked up the first egg just as the koel returned to defend her eggs. The koel saw what was going on.

The crow was bigger than her. 'Don't go too far,' the crow sneered. 'I'll be back for the rest of them.' The koel flew straight at the crow. With her beak, she broke the egg the crow held in her beak. Then the koel swooped down on the rest of her own eggs and broke them, one by one.

The commotion woke up Aviana, queen goddess of the birds. She looked down and saw what had happened. She decided that the crow would now be black forever and that the koel should never mind her own eggs.

WHY CROWS ARE BLACK

Version 3

One day Mahadev looked down upon the earth and saw a very dirty sight. There was muck all over because of which he could barely see the beautiful trees, water and mountains he had created.

But here and there in the muck he saw dozens of crows flitting around, alighting, clearing as much muck as they could.

Mahadev was amazed, even more so when he saw what they did with the pickings. He noticed that they perched on trees, cocked their heads and looked around for a place where they might deposit them without defacing the earth.

And every time they came to the same conclusion—that there was no such place on the whole earth. So they did what they had to—they ate the muck. Mahadev himself had drunk poison to save the gods. The crows were doing the same work to save man.

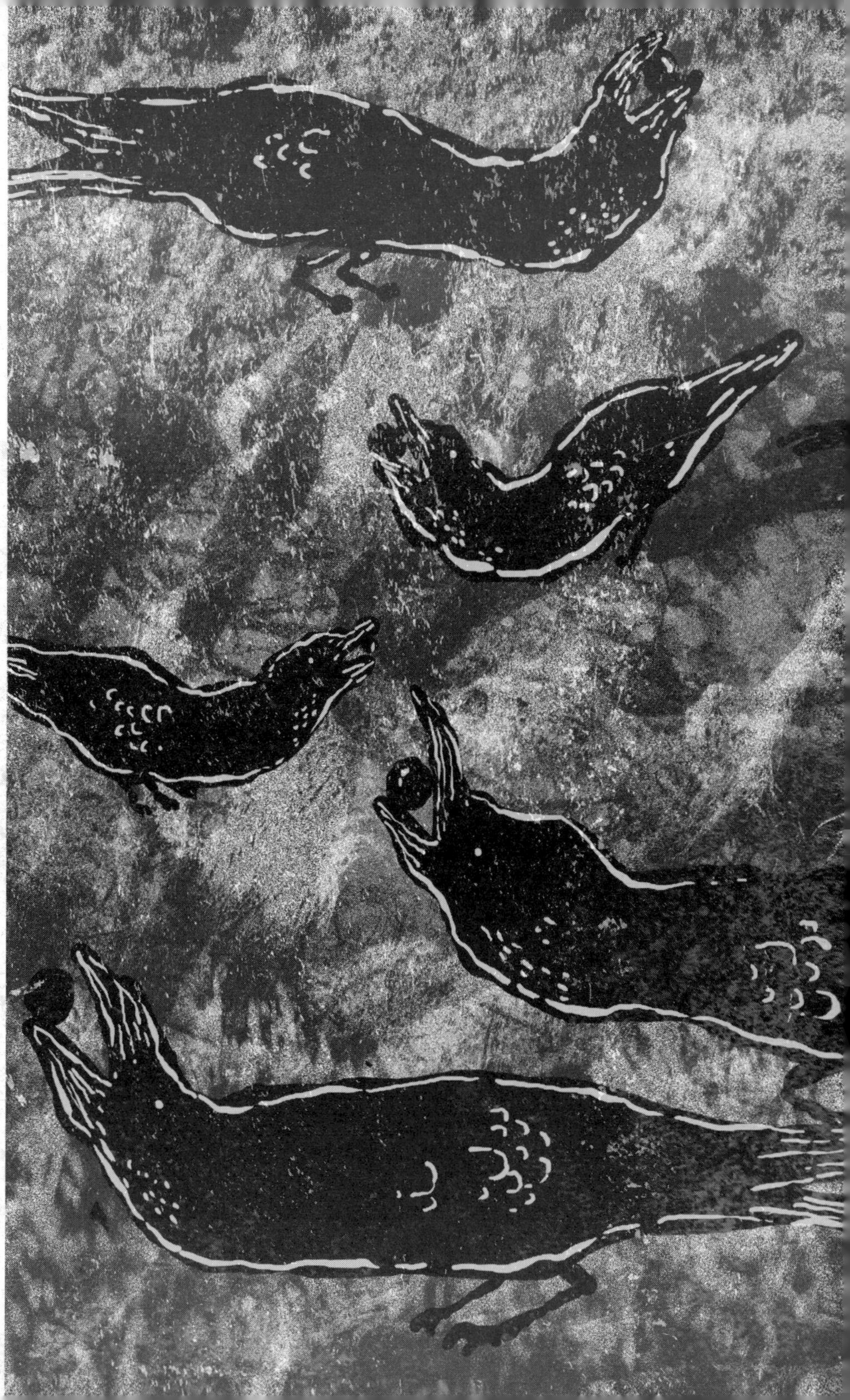

Thanks to Shanta Gokhale, who told me this story when I was a little boy of 43.

Saawri liked the stories but they did not help. Instead her dreams became more and more insistent, until finally one night, she did not dream of the egg, she did not dream of the cracking of the shell; she dreamt of blood and a white crow lying broken and still.
The dream was electrifying. Even before she was fully awake, she cawed the death caw.
Dusqui took it up. Peat followed. And Negra. In a few seconds, the whole tree was cawing the spirit of their dead comrade into the Vast Hereafter.
CAW CAW CAW CAW CAW
Noir opened an eye...
Why are we chanting? Who is dead?
The other birds fell silent. Then Peat spoke...
Saawri started it.
No one has died, but I had a dream. In it, I saw my baby come to life. In it, I saw my baby die.

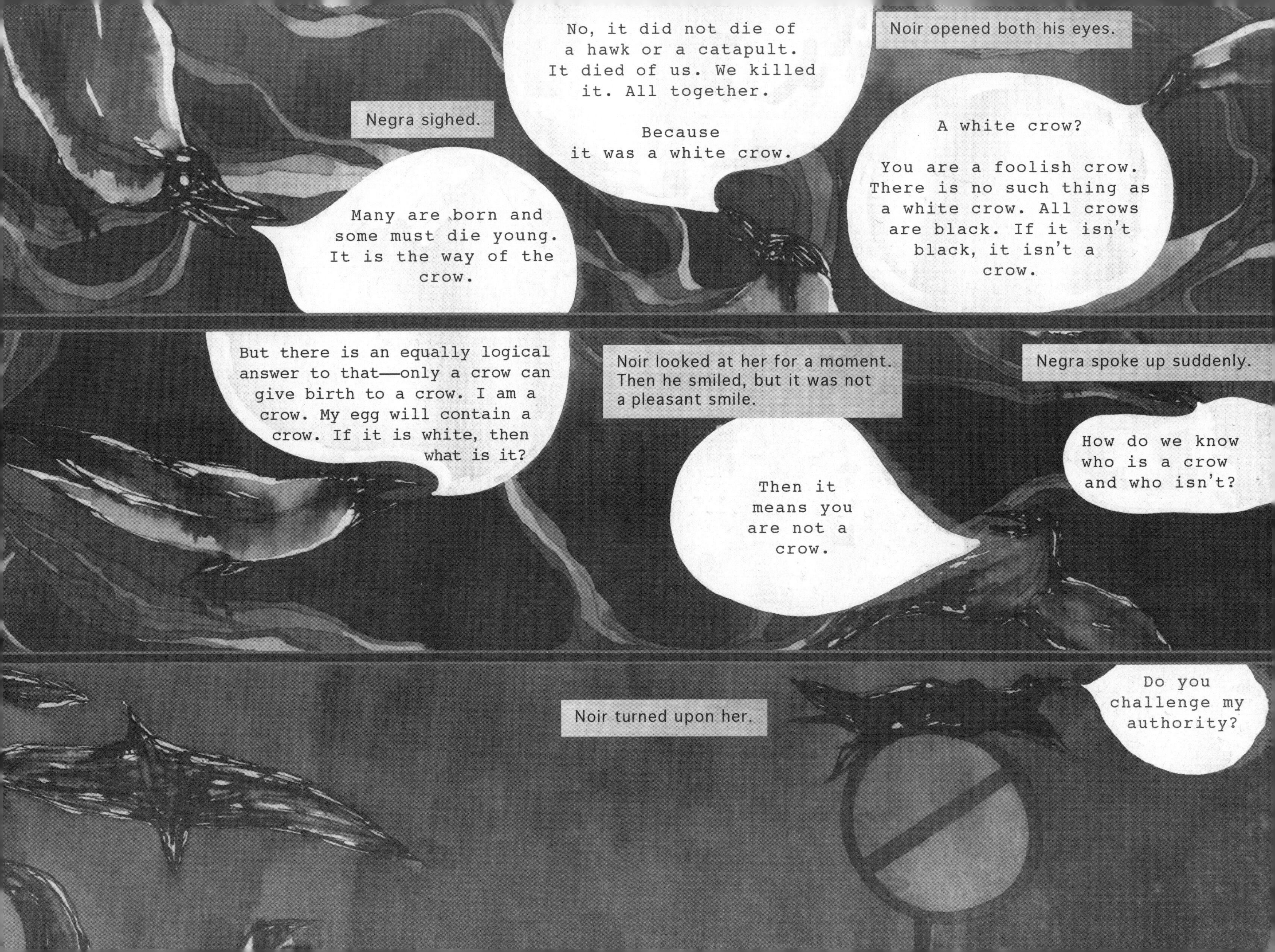
Negra sighed.
Many are born and some must die young. It is the way of the crow.
No, it did not die of a hawk or a catapult. It died of us. We killed it. All together.
Because it was a white crow.
Noir opened both his eyes.
A white crow?
You are a foolish crow. There is no such thing as a white crow. All crows are black. If it isn't black, it isn't a crow.
But there is an equally logical answer to that—only a crow can give birth to a crow. I am a crow. My egg will contain a crow. If it is white, then what is it?
Noir looked at her for a moment. Then he smiled, but it was not a pleasant smile.
Then it means you are not a crow.
Negra spoke up suddenly.
How do we know who is a crow and who isn't?
Noir turned upon her.
Do you challenge my authority?

Negra refused to be cowed.
No. I am asking my leader a question. If you say that Saawri is not a crow, then who is a crow?
A crow is black, you say. Saawri is black. A crow flies beautifully, you say. Saawri can do barrel rolls in mid-air.
A crow can think more than other birds can, you say. Saawri asks questions. What makes her not a crow?
Noir looked stumped. At this point, Peat spoke up.
A crow is one of us. If you are not with us, you are against us. If you are against us, you are not a crow.
And some of the members of the murder began to flex their wings threateningly.
I am not against you. How can I be against the murder into which I was born?
I am only asking you, what if a crow is born white?

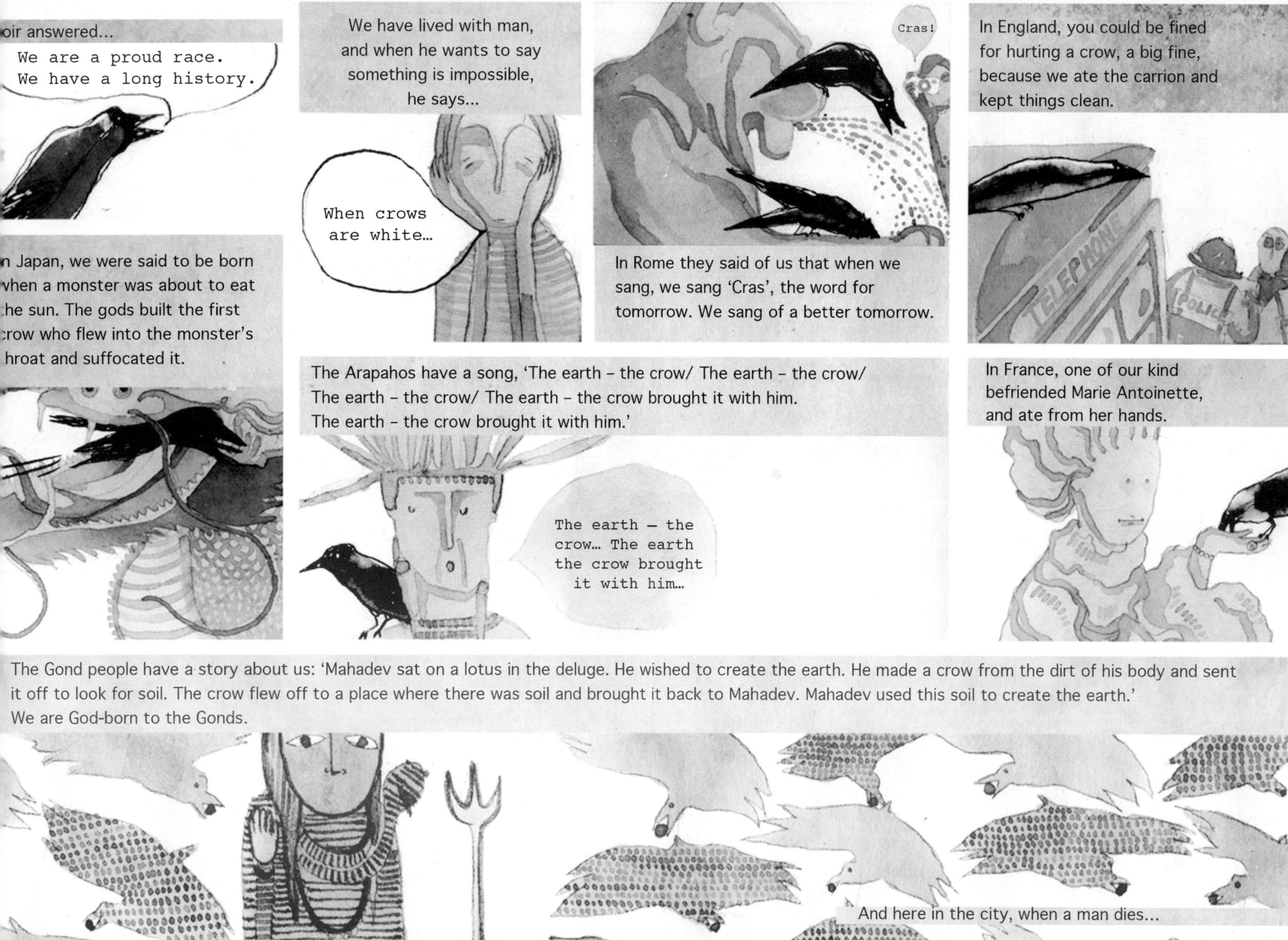
oir answered...
We are a proud race. We have a long history.
We have lived with man, and when he wants to say something is impossible, he says...
When crows are white...
Cras!
In Rome they said of us that when we sang, we sang 'Cras', the word for tomorrow. We sang of a better tomorrow.
In England, you could be fined for hurting a crow, a big fine, because we ate the carrion and kept things clean.
TELEPHONE
POLICE
n Japan, we were said to be born vhen a monster was about to eat he sun. The gods built the first row who flew into the monster's hroat and suffocated it.
The Arapahos have a song, 'The earth – the crow/ The earth – the crow/ The earth – the crow/ The earth – the crow brought it with him. The earth – the crow brought it with him.'
The earth – the crow... The earth the crow brought it with him...
In France, one of our kind befriended Marie Antoinette, and ate from her hands.
The Gond people have a story about us: 'Mahadev sat on a lotus in the deluge. He wished to create the earth. He made a crow from the dirt of his body and sent it off to look for soil. The crow flew off to a place where there was soil and brought it back to Mahadev. Mahadev used this soil to create the earth.' We are God-born to the Gonds.
And here in the city, when a man dies...

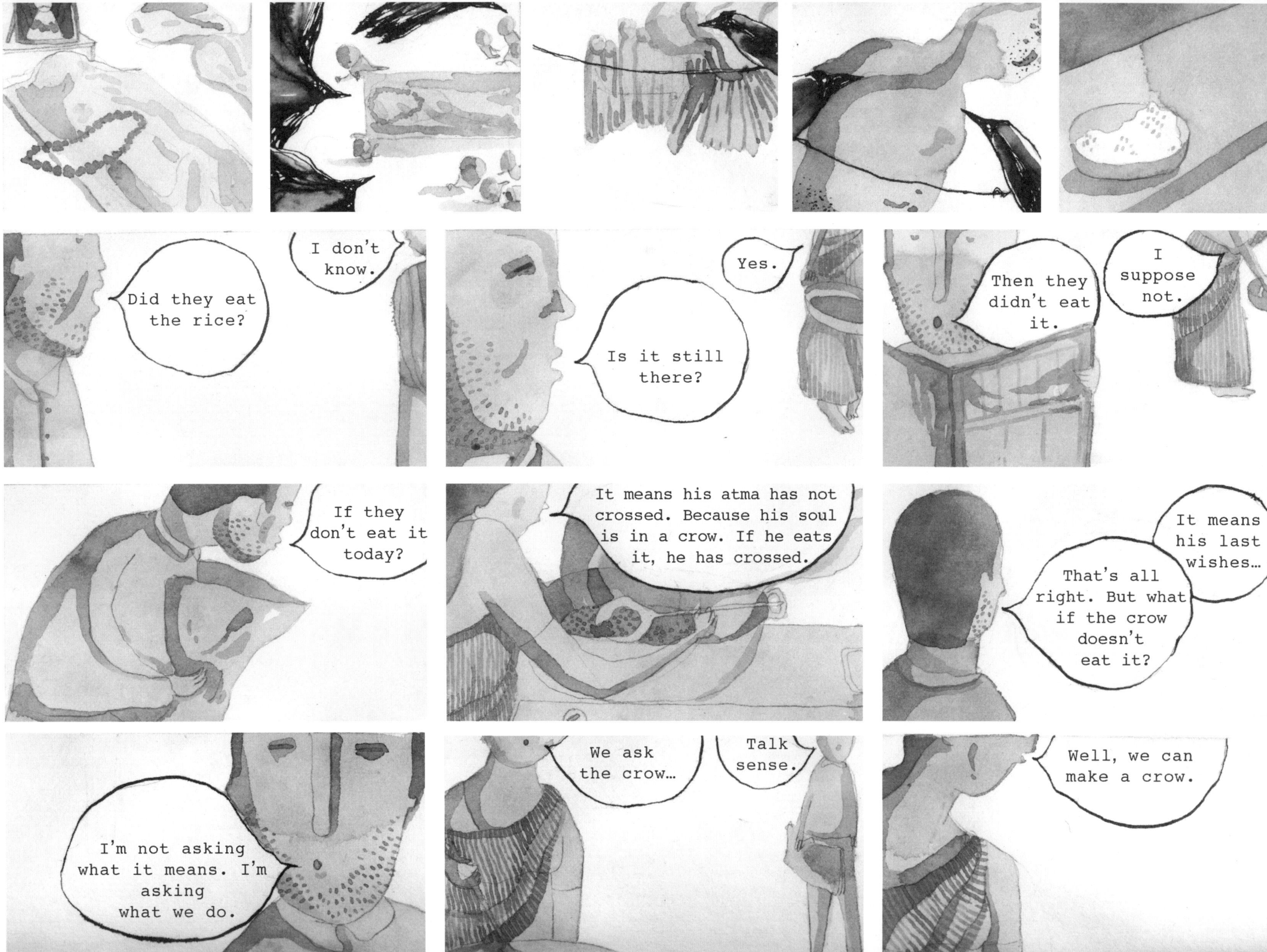
Did they eat the rice?
I don't know.
Is it still there?
Yes.
Then they didn't eat it.
I suppose not.
If they don't eat it today?
It means his atma has not crossed. Because his soul is in a crow. If he eats it, he has crossed.
It means his last wishes...
That's all right. But what if the crow doesn't eat it?
I'm not asking what it means. I'm asking what we do.
We ask the crow...
Talk sense.
Well, we can make a crow.

oir made a
ronouncement.
What will happen to this reputation of ours?
If we can't even remain the colour we are supposed to be? If a crow is not black, it must die.
shudder rippled through the tree. It ran through Saawri. It ran through some of the other crows. But Peat looked as if he agreed. So did many others.
aawri had questions
or Negra.
Why would they be happy to see a crow die?
A crow they do not even know? A crow they might love?
Negra knew the reason.
It seems to be the nature of the beast. Anything different is hated.
Your best bet would be to build your nest in another tree, a pigeon tree.
The pigeons will hate it. They'll dirty up my nest.
But they won't kill your chick before it can fly. And I'll try and help.
Saawri thought about this for a while, but she could not believe it was a solution.
It means I'm running away.
I must have my chick here and it must grow up here and it must be accepted here.
Liliar sighed.
You might have some support though.

That evening as Saawri was pressing some human hair down into the bottom of her nest to make it soft for her eggs, she felt two or three crows gather around. She looked up. Dusqui and Shabakhair and Soot were smiling at her.
Yes?
Dusqui began...
We've formed an association to help you. We're called the Whiter Feathers Club. We think white is lovely.
We want to be fairer ourselves. We believe we should all find some fairness cream tubes and see if they work on us. Then we could get others to see that white is lovely.
Saawri was unsure.
I don't know...
Soot tried to convince her.
I hate my colour. I want to be fair. And it would be lovely to have a white crow. Just lovely. I would so love the little one. I want to be an aunt. You must let me be an aunt.
It was Shabakhair's turn.
It's all very well to say we've always been black. But you know I read somewhere that there were moths in the countryside once that were white because the trees had white barks. Then the factories came and the smoke came and the tree barks turned black so the moths turned black. Now if moths can turn black, why can't crows turn white?

A cough startled all of them. It was Liliar.
I don't think the challenge is whether Saawri's child is black or white. The challenge is whether we can see it for what it is: one of us, a crow, but with a difference.
Can we accept this little one for what he or she is? Can we like her because she is kind? Can we dislike her because she is proud or rude? Can we look past the colour of the feathers?
Shabakhair fluffed her feathers up and sniffed.
Well, if you don't want our help, you only have to say so. I think you could do with some friends. There are lots of blood-thirsty beaks waiting for a white crow.
Saawri agreed to consider the suggestions.
Thanks, I'll let you know.
You would have thought no eggs had been hatched in the neem tree on Lady Jamshedji Road. Every eye was on Saawri's nest as she sat on her single egg. And then one day, the egg began to crack. Out came her chick. The crows passed judgement.
Look, it's not black.
Ugh, but it's not white either.
It's grey.
Is that what they call it? Anyway, it's not a crow.
Saawri waited for them to finish. Then she said...
It is a crow, it's a crow with a difference.

The End

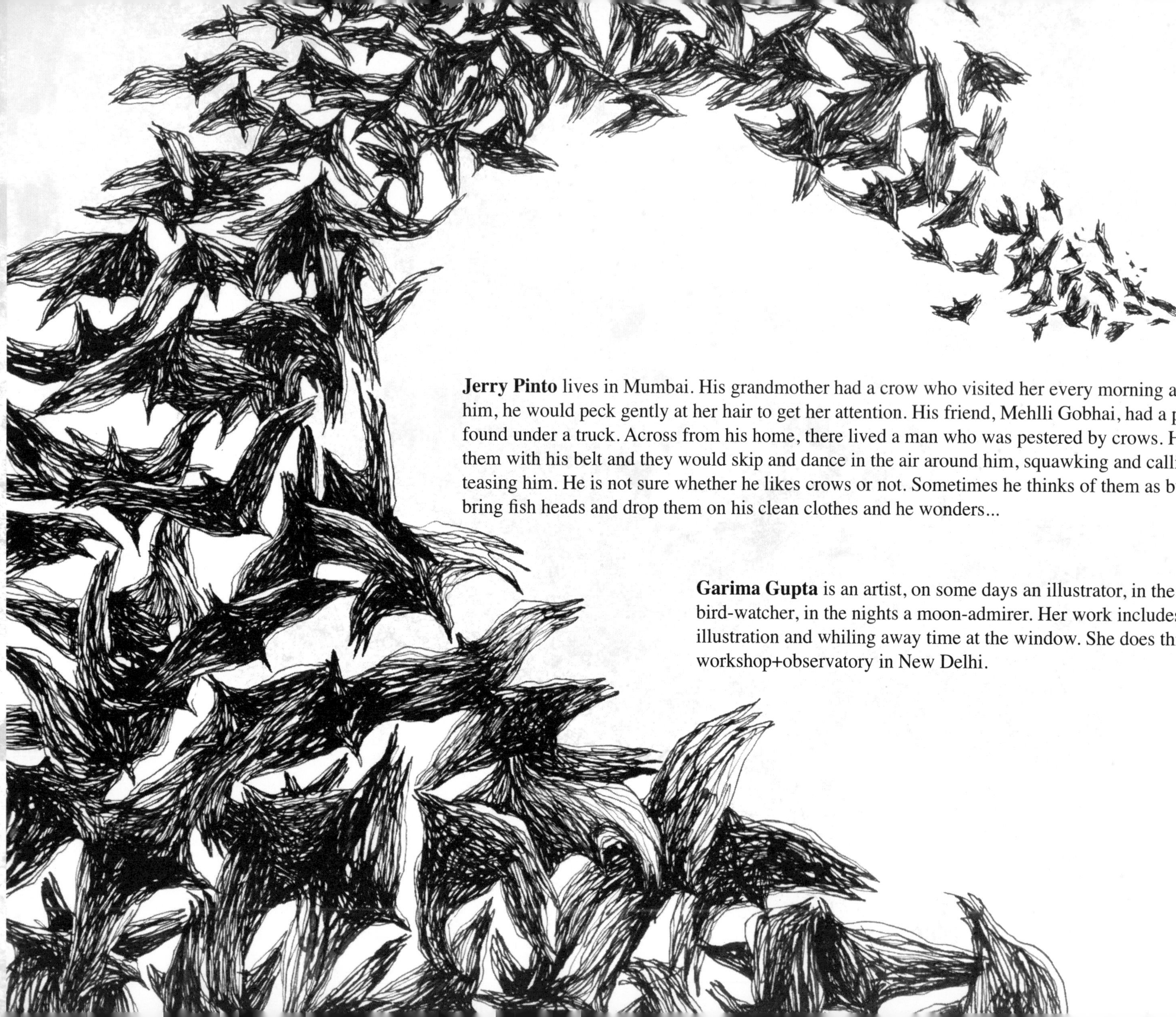

Jerry Pinto lives in Mumbai. His grandmother had a crow who visited her every morning and if she ignored him, he would peck gently at her hair to get her attention. His friend, Mehlli Gobhai, had a pet crow that he found under a truck. Across from his home, there lived a man who was pestered by crows. He would whip at them with his belt and they would skip and dance in the air around him, squawking and calling and generally teasing him. He is not sure whether he likes crows or not. Sometimes he thinks of them as buddies. Then they bring fish heads and drop them on his clean clothes and he wonders...

Garima Gupta is an artist, on some days an illustrator, in the evenings a bird-watcher, in the nights a moon-admirer. Her work includes painting, illustration and whiling away time at the window. She does this from her workshop+observatory in New Delhi.

Published by Scholastic India Pvt. Ltd.
A subsidiary of Scholastic Inc., New York, 10012 (USA).
Publishers since 1920, with international operations in Canada, Australia, New Zealand, the United Kingdom, India, and Hong Kong.

For information regarding permission, write to:
Scholastic India Pvt. Ltd.
Golf View Corporate Tower-A, 3rd Floor,
DLF Phase V, Gurgaon 122002 (India)

First edition: June 2012
This reprint edition: march 2026

ISBN-13: 978-81-8477-857-1

Printed in India at MicroPrints India, New Delhi